A. Macpherson

Sit on the Roof and Holler

for Dominic, Anri and Andrew
Sincerest thanks to Josie Karavasil,
Michael Kelly and Diana Reed.

Sit on the Roof and Holler

Poems collected by Adrian Rumble
Illustrated by Mike Gordon

Bell & Hyman Limited London

Published 1984 by Bell & Hyman Limited, Denmark House,
37–39 Queen Elizabeth Street, London SE1 2QB.
This anthology © 1984 Bell & Hyman Limited
Illustrations © 1984 Bell & Hyman Limited

British Library Cataloguing in Publication Data
Sit on the roof and holler
　　1.　Children's poetry, English
　　I.　Rumble, Adrian
821'.914'0809282　　　PR1195.C47

ISBN 0 7135 1447 7

Typeset by Tradespools Ltd., Frome , Somerset
Printed and bound in Great Britain by
Biddles Ltd., Guildford

Contents

And we made merry work

I meant to do my work today

I meant to do my work today —
But a brown bird sang in the apple tree,
And a butterfly flitted across the field,
And all the leaves were calling me.

And the wind went sighing over the land,
Tossing the grasses to and fro,
And a rainbow held out its shining hand —
So what could I do but laugh and go?

Richard le Gallienne

Engineers

Pistons, valves and wheels and gears
That's the life of engineers
Thumping, chunking engines going
Hissing steam and whistles blowing.

There's not a place I'd rather be
Than working round machinery
Listening to that clanking sound
Watching all the wheels go round.

Jimmy Garthwaite

Song of the Washing Machine

Rolling them round,
Rolling them round,
Nothing else does it but
Rolling them round.

Swishing them clean,
Swishing them clean,
Some of those stockings
Weren't fit to be seen!

Spinning them dry,
Spinning them dry,
When you know how
It's as easy as pie!

When the job's over,
With nobody by it,
The Washing Machine
Is suddenly quiet.

Donald Mattam

Washing day

A washing machine
A sploshing machine
Splish, splash, splosh.
Whenever I use my washing machine
It splishes and splashes
All over the floor,
It splashes and sploshes
As far as the door.
I get into muddles
And step into puddles,
I don't think I'll use it
Any more.

Anne English

Oh, who will wash the tiger's ears?

Oh, who will wash the tiger's ears?
And who will comb his tail?
And who will brush his sharp white teeth?
And who will file his nails?

Oh, Bobby may wash the tiger's ears
And Susy may file his nails
And Lucy may brush his long white teeth
And I'll go down for the mail.

Shel Silverstein

16

The head came off my hammer today

The head came off my hammer today,
I put it back on without delay,
Then as I was pulling a big nail out,
The head stayed on but the handle came out.

P. H. Kilby

The Do-It-Yourself Song

Sandpaper, screwdriver, chisel and screws,
Brushes, all sizes for me to choose.
Jam jars and packets, bottles and tins,
Everything waiting for me to begin.
Scraper and paintbrush, hammer and nails,
Sweeping brush, scrubbing brush, water in pails,
Ceiling and walls, cupboard and shelf,
This is the song of the Do-It-Yourself.

Anne English

The digging song

In your hands you hold the spade,
Feel its well-worn wood,
Now you drive it in the earth,
Drive it deep and good.

    Dig dig digging dirt,
    Dirt inside your vest.
    Did dig digging dirt,
    Digging dirt is best.

Here are worms that twist and loop
Tight as knots in string,
Here are spiders, ants and bugs
Running in a ring.

    Dig dig digging dirt,
    Dirt inside your vest.
    Dig dig digging dirt,
    Digging dirt is best.

Soon your hands are red and raw,
Blisters on the way,
But your spade just wants to dig
All the long, hot day.

Dig dig digging dirt,
Dirt inside your vest.
Dig dig digging dirt,
Digging dirt is best.

Wes Magee

A choice

There's lots of ways of doing things,
As everyone supposes,
For some turn up their sleeves at work
And some turn up their noses.

Anon

A little girl

When I was a little girl
    About seven years old
I hadn't got a petticoat
    To keep me from the cold.

So I went into Darlington,
    That pretty little town,
And there I bought a petticoat,
    A cloak, and a gown.

I went into the woods
   And built me a kirk,
And all the birds of the air
   They helped me to work.

The hawk with his long claws,
   Pulled down the stone,
The dove with her rough bill,
   Brought me them home.

The parrot was the clergyman,
   The peacock was the clerk,
The bullfinch played the organ,
   And we made merry work.

Traditional song

Unwilling

Mum said, Polish,
Dad said, Dust,
I said, If
I must,
I must,
But I would rather go and play
And do the work another day.

Helen Russell

Creepy crawly caterpillar

Bees

Every bee
that
ever was
was
partly
sting
and partly
. . . buzz.

Jack Prelutsky

Fly

I
really
cannot
learn to hate
the
fly
that walks
around my plate.

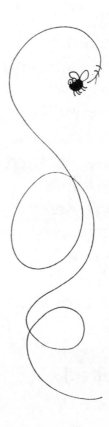

I
know
flies carry
germs
and
things
but
oh
they have
such
busy wings
and DON'T have stings.

Peggy Dunstan

Blue Butterfly

Butterfly,
Blue Butterfly,
all your playground
is the sky,
all your world's
a blaze-of-colour —
blue, rose, emerald,
nothing duller;
touching roses
with your wings,
rising where
a skylark sings
from the garden
to the sky,
there you go,
Blue Butterfly.

Ivy O. Eastwick

Caterpillar

Creepy crawly caterpillar
Looping up and down,
Furry tufts of hair along
Your back of golden brown.

You will soon be wrapped in silk,
Asleep for many a day;
And then, a handsome butterfly,
You'll stretch and fly away.

Mary Dawson

Mumbling bees

All around the garden flowers
Big velvet bees are bumbling,
They hover low and as they go
They're mumbling, mumbling, mumbling.

To lavender and snapdragons
The busy bees keep coming,
And all the busy afternoon
They're humming, humming, humming.

Inside each bell-shaped flower and rose
They busily go stumbling,
Collecting pollen all day long
And bumbling, bumbling, bumbling.

Daphne Lister

Wasps

Wasps in brightly
Coloured vests,
Chewing wood,
To make their nests.

Wasps, like rockets,
Zooming high,
Then dropping down
Where peaches lie.

Anne Ruddick

Ladybird

No button so shiny,
So coloured, so tiny;
No bead was ever
So lively and bright.
I see with delight
This brooch that no finger
Ever pinned on;
I want it to linger,
But, see, it takes flight
And now it has gone.

Donald Mattam

Summer afternoon

Bumble bee so busy
Round the hollyhocks,
Working all the summer
In your furry socks,
Don't you wish that you could
Have a holiday?
Busy, buzzy, Bumble,
Don't you ever play?

Cynthia Mitchell

Old Sam Snail

Old Sam Snail, met a great big thrush.
'Can't stop now,' said Sam, 'I'm in an awful rush.'
But Sam couldn't creep any faster than a crawl,
So the big thrush swallowed him in no time at all.

Jenny Cornelius

Under a stone where the earth was firm

Under a stone where the earth was firm,
I found a wriggly, wriggly worm;
'Good morning,' I said.
'How are you today?'
But the wriggly worm just wriggled away!

Anon

A bit of jungle in the street

The city mouse and the garden mouse

The city mouse lives in a house;
The garden mouse lives in a bower,
He's friendly with the frogs and toads,
And sees the pretty plants in flower.

The city mouse eats bread and cheese;
The garden mouse eats what he can;
We will not grudge him seeds and stocks,
Poor little timid furry man.

Christina Rossetti

Alley cat

A bit of jungle in the street
He goes on velvet toes,
And slinking through the shadows, stalks
Imaginary foes.

Esther Valck Georges

Sardines

A baby Sardine
Saw her first submarine:
She was scared and watched through a peephole.

'Oh, come, come, come,'
Said the Sardine's mum,
'It's only a tin full of people.'

Spike Milligan

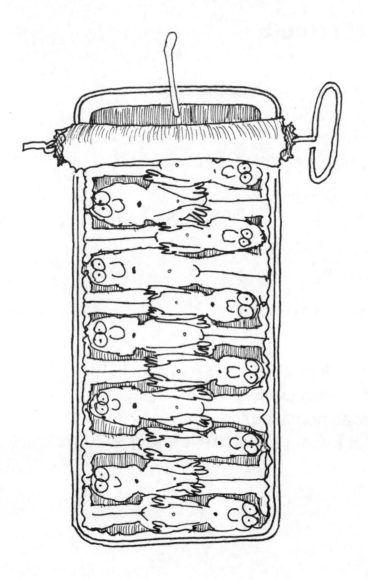

Sabretooth

Sabretooth, oh Sabretooth,
You really are spectacular.
Sabretooth, oh Sabretooth,
You're very like Count Dracula.

Tom Stanier

The elephant

The elephant carries a great big trunk;
He never packs it with clothes;
It has no lock and it has no key,
But he takes it wherever he goes,

Anon

The mammoth

The mammoth is strong,
The mammoth is brave.
But dear, oh dear,
He could do with a shave.

Tom Stanier

Two little brown Bears

Two little brown Bears
lived in a wood –
one was bad,
the other was good.

One went every day
to school –
the other went fishing
in Blackberry Pool.

One learned Add-up
and Take-away –
the other spent all of
HIS time in play.

One ate up his
prunes-and-rice
and always said 'Thank you.
Very nice.'

The other said:
'PRUNES? Oh, what a bore'
and emptied his plate
on the kitchen floor.

One helped his mother
when school was done –
the other chased little boys
just for fun.

If YOU were a little Bear
living in a wood,
would you be bad?
or would you be good?

Ivy O. Eastwick

My dog

If I had a dog his ears would flop,
His tail would be waggly and white at the top,
His eyes would be brown, and the glint in them
   white,
We would gaze at the stars, and he'd bark at the
   night.

If I had a dog we'd be friends together,
Going for journeys through all sorts of weather.
In the ice, in the snow, in the red winter light,
We'd walk on forever, and he'd bark at the night.

Clive Riche

Jump

'Jump! Jump!'
Said the kangaroo.
And everyone jumped.
What a thump!
What a bump!
What an earth shaking,
Window breaking
Jaggeroo.
'Fine! Fine!' said the kangaroo.
'Let's do it again!'

Olive Dove

Katey

I really don't know what they'd do at the zoo
If it wasn't for Katey the kangaroo;
She works very hard but she doesn't get paid
As she cares for the children who get mislaid.
They sit in her pouch and they travel around,
And wait till their mothers and fathers are found;
I really don't know what they'd do at the zoo
If it wasn't for Katey the kangaroo.

Roland Egan

Six little mice

Six little mice sat down to spin,
Pussy passed by, and she peeped in.
'What are you at, my little men?'
'Making coats for gentlemen.'
'Shall I come in and bite off your threads?'
'No, no, Miss Pussy, you'll snip off our heads.'
'Oh, no, I'll not, I'll help you to spin.'
'That may be so, but you don't come in!'

Anon

Higglety, pigglety, pop

Higglety, pigglety, pop!
The dog has eaten the mop;
The pig's in a hurry,
The cat's in a flurry,
Higglety, pigglety, pop!

Anon

I once had a dog

I once had a dog
That had no sense;
He ran round the house
And barked at the fence.

Anon

Comes a bird of paradise

Hen's song

Chick, chick, come out of your shell,
I've warmed you long and I've warmed you well;
The sun is hot and the sky is blue
Quick, chick, it's time you came through.

Rose Fyleman

Strawberry patch

Strawberry-picking!
strawberry-picking!
Jonno and Jane
went strawberry-picking
out in my garden
steeped in dew
where scarlet-and-crimson
strawberries grew.

Two for the basket
or maybe three,
then one for Jonno
and Jane and me;
three for the basket
once again
then – another for Jonno
and me and Jane.

While the Starlings make
a terrible fuss:
'Don't gather them all,
leave SOME for US!'

Ivy O. Eastwick

Louder than sparrows

Singing, singing,
all the world is singing —
sparrows on the housetops,
thrushes in the trees,
bees above the hawthorn
crickets in the clover,
and, loudest of them all, sings
   JANE-SARAH LEAS,
louder than the sparrows,
sweeter than the thrushes,
chirpier than the crickets,
bolder than the bees,
listen! and you'll hear her,
singing to the whole world,
singing with the springtime
underneath the trees.

Ivy O. Eastwick

Catch

For a scattering of wheat,
Just a handful of corn,
Come the sparrows of the street
And the peacocks of the lawn;

For a pocketful of money
And a scattering of rice
And a promise sweet as honey
Comes a bird of paradise.

Cynthia Mitchell

Four wrens

There were two wrens upon a tree,
Whistle and I'll come to thee;
Another came and there were three,
Whistle and I'll come to thee;
Another came and there were four,
You needn't whistle any more,
For being frightened, off they flew,
And there are none to show to you.

Anon

I wish I had a pony

Shop

If I were a shop, I'm sure I'd stock
The most beautiful things in the world.
I'd have counters for rainbows, and buckets of dew,
And shelves full of mountains, and bottles of view,
Fountains and forests and sets of green seas,
And bouquets of sunshine, and spray cans of
   breeze.

Clive Riche

Want a penny?

Want a penny?
Haven't got any.

Want a nickel?
Buy a pickle.

Want a dime?
Some other time.

Want a quarter?
Jump in the water.

Want a dollar?
Sit on the roof and holler.

Traditional American

I wish I had a pony

I wish I had a pony
with a gold and silver mane
I'd ride him in the sunshine
I'd ride him in the rain
I'd ride him to the moon and back
and gallop around the sun
I wouldn't take him home again
until the day was done.

P. H. Kilby

It's only a penny

It's only a penny,
To Abergavenny,
It's twopence to go
Up to Troon,
So maybe next year,
If it isn't too dear,
I'll save up,
And go to the moon.

Helen Russell

Up in the air

Zooming across the sky,
Like a great bird you fly,
    Aeroplane,
    Silvery white
    In the light.

Turning and twisting in the air,
When shall I ever be there,
    Aeroplane,
    Piloting you
    Far in the blue?

James S. Tippett

Starlight

Starlight, star bright,
First star I see tonight,
I wish I may, I wish I might,
Have the wish I wish tonight.

Anon

Now put this parsnip on your nose

Breakfast

Sausages, sausages sizzling in the pan;
eggs flipping and a-flopping,
catch them if you can!

Porridge, porridge bubbling on the stove,
slurping and a-glurping,
that's the food I love!

Bacon crinkling, wrinkling at the edges;
toast browning and a-burning,
popping out the toaster
in great fat wedges!

Tangy bitter marmalade
with chewy lumps of peel.
That's the breakfast that I like –
the day's best meal!

Adrian Rumble

Why did the children

'Why did the children
put beans in their ears
when the one thing we told the children
they must not do
was put beans in their ears?'

'Why did the children
pour molasses on the cat
when the one thing we told the children
they must not do
was pour molasses on the cat?'

Carl Sandburg

Teddy Bear

Teddy Bear
Sat on a chair,
With ham and jam
And plum and pear.

'This is queer,'
Said Teddy Bear,
'The more I eat
The less is there!'

L. H. Allen

A thousand hairy savages

A thousand hairy savages
Sitting down to lunch
Gobble gobble glup glup
Munch munch munch.

Spike Milligan

Millicent-Margaret-Mary-Ann

Millicent-Margaret-Mary-Ann,
Lived in a house made of marzipan,
She nibbled the roof, the chimneys and wall,
She nibbled the doors, the windows and all,
And when she had eaten the whole of the house
She galloped away on a marzipan mouse.

Daphne Lister

I'm an apple

I'm a red apple.
Eat me.
Chew me and chomp me,
Sweetly.
Pick me and peel me,
But buy me, don't steal me,
For I'm a red apple,
Eat me.

I'm a green apple,
Bake me.
Into hot pies and sweet puddings
Make me.
Cut me and core me,
But please don't ignore me,
For I'm a green apple,
Bake me.

I'm a gold apple.
Leave me.
Don't pluck me, and please don't be
Greedy.
You've eaten too much,
So don't snatch and don't touch.
Let me stay in the sunlight,
Leave me.

Clive Riche

Vegetable man

Now, put this parsnip on your nose,
Some radish by your cheek,
Upon your chest an artichoke
And in your hand a leek,
Between the toes place Brussels sprouts,
Cucumbers on your knee,
Brown bread and butter on your head;
Then you can come to tea.

K. M. O'Connor

Gee up, Neddy, to the fair

Gee up, Neddy, to the fair;
What shall we buy when we get there?
A penny apple and a penny pear;
Gee up, Neddy, to the fair.

Anon

Porridge is bubbling

Porridge is bubbling,
Bubbling hot,
Stir it round
And round in the pot.
The bubbles plip!
The bubbles plop!
It's ready to eat
All bubbling hot.

Anon

Breakfast

Good morning little earthworm
said the speckled Thrush
Where would you be going
so early in a rush
I'm off to find some breakfast
he answered with a frown
Well so am I sir said the Thrush
and quickly gulped him down.

P. H. Kilby

The bakers

Auntie Amy made some scones
But they were hard as cobblestones.

Cousin Constance baked a cake
And we all thought our teeth would break!

Sister Susan made some bread –
Every loaf was heavy as lead.

But when my Mum makes treacle pud
You've never tasted one as good!

Daphne Lister

One day a boy went walking

One day a boy went walking,
And walked into a store.
He bought a pound of sausages
And laid them on the floor.

The boy began to whistle
He whistled up a tune,
And all the little sausages
Danced around the room.

Anon

When I am the President

When I am the President
Of the United States,
I'll eat up all the candy
And swing on all the gates.

Anon

Pancakes

Mix a pancake,
Stir a pancake,
Pop it in the pan.
Fry the pancake,
Toss the pancake,
Catch it if you can.

Christina Rossetti

Advice

Eat up your crusts,
And your hair will grow curly,
It's good for your teeth,
And you'll always rise early.

My Dad tells me that,
But his hair is straight,
His teeth are all false,
And he's always up late.

Helen Russell

The bells of Northampton

Roast beef and marshmallows,
Say the bells of All Hallows.
Pancakes and fritters,
Say the bells of St Peter's.
Roast beef and boiled,
Say the bells of St. Giles'.
Poker and tongs,
Say the bells of St. John's.

Traditional English

Salt, mustard, vinegar, pepper

Salt, mustard, vinegar, pepper,
French almond rock,
Bread and butter for your supper
That's all mother's got.
Fish and chips and coca cola,
Put them in a pan,
Irish stew and ice cream soda,
We'll eat all we can.

78

Salt, mustard, vinegar, pepper,
French almond rock,
Bread and butter for your supper
That's all mother's got.
Eggs and bacon, salted herring,
Put them in a pot,
Pickled onions, apple pudding,
We will eat the lot.

Salt, mustard, vinegar, pepper,
Pig's head and trout,
Bread and butter for your supper
OUT spells out.

Traditional English

Reward

When Jacky's a good boy,
    He shall have cakes and custard;
But when he does nothing but cry,
    He shall have nothing but mustard.

Anon

Hannah Bantry

Hannah Bantry,
In the pantry,
Gnawing at a mutton bone;
How she gnawed it,
How she clawed it,
When she found herself alone.

Anon

Some dye their hair pink

Open windows

The windows are open at Number One,
And Dick the canary sings in the sun.

On her piano, little Miss Moore
Practises scales at Number Four.

A kettle is whistling at Number Ten.
Old Mother Moon's making tea again.

At Number Sixteen young Jenny is in;
There's her transistor's happy din!

The window at Number Eighteen is wide;
You can hear Mrs. Chadwick coughing inside.

Tapping his typewriter all the day through,
Mr. Gray's working at Twenty-two.

But here's Thirty-three. We hurry on past.
The curtains are drawn and the windows shut fast.

It's dark and unfriendly, cheerless and chill
— And a lean cat sleeps on the window-sill.

Alexander Franklin

The old fellow

There was an old fellow
who lived by the sea
crying 'O sir! There's no one
so happy as me!
For when in, sir, and out, sir,
the ocean it goes
I have always the sand, sir,
to tickle my toes!'

This cheery old fellow
who lived by the beach
would say over and over:
'It's easy to teach!
For when out, sir, and in, sir,
the ocean it flows,
one has always the salt, sir,
to sniff up one's nose!'

Jean Kenward

I had a little brother

I had a little brother
His name was Tiny Tim
I put him in the bathtub
To teach him how to swim
He drank up all the water
He ate up all the soap
He died last night
With a bubble in his throat
In came the doctor
In came the nurse
In came the lady
With the alligator purse
Dead said the doctor
Dead said the nurse
Dead said the lady
With the alligator purse
Out went the doctor
Out went the nurse
Out went the lady
With the alligator purse.

Traditional English

The girl in the mirror

I looked in the mirror and what did I see?
Another wee person, looking at me!
She smiles when I smile, looks cross when I do,
We must be very alike, we two.
Her hair is like mine, her nose is too.
Her eyes like mine, are coloured blue.
But I noticed that if I shut my right eye,
She shuts her left. I can't think why.

Jenny Cornelius

Little Arabella Miller

Little Arabella Miller
Found a woolly caterpillar.
First it crawled upon her mother,
Then upon her baby brother;
All said, 'Arabella Miller
Take away that caterpillar.'

Ann Elliott

Little Dick

Little Dick,
He was so quick,
He tumbled over the timber,
He bent his bow,
To shoot a crow,
And shot the cat in the winder.

Traditional American

The mystery creatures

They dwell on a planet not far from the Sun.
Some fly through the sky, while others just run.

Some have big heads which are hairless as tin,
While others have hair which sprouts from their
    skin.

They dig food from dirt, and gobble dead meat.
The young squeal like pigs if you tickle their feet.

They slurp, burp, and grunt; their manners are bad.
Their eyes become waterfalls when they feel sad.

They come in most colours – some yellow, some
    white
Some dye their hair pink and DO look a sight.

These creatures vary from titchy to tall,
and in salty water they've been known to crawl.

Well, who are these creatures? Can't you guess
    who?
The answer is easy; it's you, you, and YOU.

Wes Magee

The clown

I like to see
The spotted clown
Throwing dishes
In the air.
When they've started
Coming down
He looks as though
He didn't care,
But catches each one
Perfectly,
Over and over,
Everytime,
One and two and
One-two-three-
Like a pattern
Or a rhyme.

Dorothy Aldis

Just like me

I went up one pair of stairs.
    JUST LIKE ME.

I went up two pairs of stairs.
    JUST LIKE ME.

I went into a room.
    JUST LIKE ME.

I looked out of the window.
    JUST LIKE ME.

And there I saw a monkey.
    JUST LIKE ME.

Anon

A piper

A piper in the streets today
Set up and tuned, and started to play,
And away, away, away on the tide
Of his music we started; on every side
Doors and windows were opened wide,
And men left down their work and came,
And women with petticoats coloured like flame
And little bare feet that were blue with cold,
Went dancing back to the age of gold,
And all the world went gay, went gay,
For half an hour in the street to-day.

Seumas O'Sullivan

Step on a crack

Step on a crack,
You'll break your mother's back;
Step on a line,
You'll break your father's spine.

Step in a ditch,
Your mother's nose will itch;
Step in the dirt,
You'll tear your father's shirt.

Traditional American

from: **Greer County**

How happy am I when I crawl into bed –
A rattlesnake hisses a tune at my head,
A gay little centipede, all without fear,
Crawls over my pillow and into my ear.

My clothes is all ragged as my language is rough,
My bread is corn-dodgers, both solid and tough;
But yet I am happy, and live at my ease
On sorghum molasses, bacon, and cheese.

Traditional American

Space-men

What do space-men eat?
What do space-men wear?
How do space-men sleep?
And do they comb their hair?

Can they walk about?
Or do they curl up small?
Do they speak or shout?
Or never talk at all?

What's a satellite?
Are there rocks up there?
How do rockets shoot?
How, and when, and where?

Anne Ruddick

How high can you jump?

Inside

Inside the large box
A smaller box.
Inside the smaller box
A very small box.
Inside the very small box
ME
  AND
    I
      WANT
        TO
          GET
            OUT.

Olive Dove

Ten tom-toms

Ten tom-toms,
Timpany, too,
Ten tall tubas
And an old kazoo.

Ten trombones –
Give them a hand!
The sitting-standing-marching-running
Big Brass Band.

Anon

On my little guitar

On my little guitar
With only one string
I play in the moonlight
Any old thing.

C. Louis Leipoldt – translated by A. Delius

Walking on the Moon

Hey! Look at me!
I'm walking on the Moon.
Six times lighter here am I,
I can jump six times as high
When I'm walking on the Moon!

Hey! Look at me!
I'm bouncing on the Moon.
Like a wind caught tennis ball
I feel I'll never fall
When I'm bouncing on the Moon!

Hey! Look at me!
I'm striding on the Moon.
I'm a giant in seven league boots;
A tree freed from its roots
When I'm striding on the Moon!

Hey! Look at me!
I'm floating on the Moon.
I'm defying gravity,
Dry swimming in the sea
When I'm floating on the Moon!

Adrian Rumble

Getting wet

One jump – over the seaweed!
Two jumps – for sandy toes!
Three jumps – over the pebbles,
And SPLASH! in the sea she goes!
  SPLASH!

Mary Dawson

The swing

I fly
high, high,
in the sky,
'Goodbye
passers-by,
goodbye.'
'Oh, my.'
Trees sigh
on high
while I
sail by
in the sky.
'Goodbye,
goodbye.'

Jenny Cornelius

Jumping rhyme

Jump, jump, how high can you jump?
Up to the moon and down with a bump.

Skip, skip, how far can you skip?
All round the world with never a slip.

Hop, hop, how long can you hop?
From morning to night and never stop.

Run, run, how fast can you run?
On my two feet I chase the sun.

Sleep, sleep, how long will you sleep?
From morn to night in slumber deep.

Anne English

High jump

Here's my hand,
Come jump with me,
Over the river,
Over the sea.
Small jump,
Big jump,
One, two, three,
High in the air,
And over the tree.

K. M. O'Connor

Problems

The car's on strike, so
Dad's on Mum's bike, and
Mum's on Gran's trike, and
Gran's got my roller-skates –
Whee – whizz!

Rachel Vernon

Stretching

Lying down upon the mat,
I'm s-t-r-e-t-c-h-i-n-g, like my little cat.
Arms and legs now, nice and s-l-o-w,
I can f-e-e-l my muscles grow.
Stretching, rolling, on the mat,
Exactly like my little cat.

G. M. Green

Mother, mother

Mother, may I go and bathe?
Yes, my darling daughter.
Hang your clothes on yonder tree,
But don't go near the water.

Mother, may I go to swim?
Yes, my darling daughter.
Fold your clothes up neat and trim,
But don't go near the water.

Anon

The bus ride

Bumps ... bumps ... bumps ...
My father gives me thumps ...
My mother combs
My hair and makes
Me gingerbread
And applecakes –
Bumps ... bumps ... bumps ...
My father gives me thumps!

Jean Kenward

A wide-awake bounce

Eyes like a hawk
And a nose like a beagle,
Bold as a lion
And as swift as an eagle,
Ears like a fox
And a touch like a squid
You won't catch me out –
I'm an on-the-ball kid.

Cynthia Mitchell

Kite

A kite on the ground
is just paper and string
but up in the air
it will dance and will sing.
A kite in the air
will dance and will caper
but back on the ground
is just string and paper.

Anon

No-one loves a Christmas Tree on March the twenty-fifth

Time

Mother's little watch
Goes ticka-ticka-tick,
As if it were saying,
'Be quick, be quick, be quick!'

But when Big Ben
Begins to chime
It's as if he were saying,
'Take your TIME, take your TIME!'

Daphne Lister

I saw the moon a-shining

I saw the moon a-shining
on a windy night
it blew so hard it blew so strong
it blew it out of sight
it blew it through the tree tops
it blew it down the lane
it blew it round the chimney pots
then blew it back again.

P. H. Kilby

Merry . . .

No one's hangin' stockin's up,
No one's bakin' pie,
No one's lookin' up to see
A new star in the sky.
No one's talkin' brotherhood,
No one's givin' gifts,
And no one loves a Christmas tree
On March the twenty-fifth.

Shel Silverstein

Evening red

Evening red and morning grey,
Send the traveller on his way;
Evening grey and morning red
Bring the rain upon his head.

Anon

Night lights

There is no need to light a night-light
On a light night like tonight;
For a night-light's light's a slight light
When the moonlight's white and bright.

Anon

Winter

When winter's wearing white,
Bright, diamond-studded dresses
She's as smiling and beguiling
As the fairest of princesses.

When winter's wearing grey,
Frayed, freezing foggy breeches
She's as vicious and capricious
As the wickedest of witches.

Cynthia Mitchell

The enemy

Run leaves,
Run before the wicked wind
Or he'll catch you
With his crafty reaching hands.
Run and pile up
In hollow tree and empty shed.
Lie quiet now,
Not a whisper or a crackle,
He's just outside
Waiting to grab and fling you high
And how he'll laugh
To see you whirl and toss and fly.

Jennifer Andrews

118

Summer days

I'm looking for a hot spot.
A what spot?
A hot spot.
I'm looking for a hot spot.
To lie out in the sun.
I'm looking for a hot spot
To play and have some fun.
I'm looking for a hot spot
To hit a ball and run.
Oh, I'm looking for a hot spot.
A what spot?
A hot spot.
I'm looking for a hot spot
Now summer has begun.

Anne English

Sledging

Look at us
As we go
Sledging on the bright white snow.

Faces beaming
Long hair streaming
Passing those who are too slow.

Wendy Elizabeth Johnson

A pocket full of honey

The biggest firework

The biggest firework
Ever lit,
Fizzed, banged,
Glittered, flew
In Golden-Silver-
Red-Green-Blue.
It rocketed
So far away,
It brought to night
A burst of day,
Electric bulbs
A million bright
Of shining spray.

But of its fiery magic spell
All that is left
Is the smoke smell . . .

Anon

122

The sea's treasures

In swept the sea
With a swirl and a swish,
It shimmered and whispered,
'Choose what you wish.'

And the sea showed its treasures
At the edge of the shore,
Shining bright pebbles
And shells by the score.

Long ribbons of seaweed
That shone gold and red,
'I'll share them, I'll share,'
The sea softly said.

Daphne Lister

123

Look

Look up, look up,
Apples are red
And ripe and waiting to drop,
Look up, look far,
Swallows are swirling,
Zig-zag diving and turning,
Look – look high,
The slim brown lark
Is flinging and winging, up –
Up – up – up and away.

Jennifer Andrews

Scene

Little trees like pencil strokes
black and still
etched forever in my mind
on that snowy hill.

Charlotte Zolotow

A spike of green

When I went out
The sun was hot,
It shone upon
My flower pot.

And there I saw
A spike of green
That no one else
Had ever seen!

On other days
The things I see
Are mostly old
Except for me.

But this green spike
So new and small
Had never yet
Been seen at all.

Barbara Baker

Sing a sing of pockets

Sing a song of pockets
A pocket full of stones
A pocket full of feathers
Or maybe chicken bones
A pocket full of bottle tops
A pocket full of money
Or if it's something sweet you want
A pocket full of honey . . .
Ugh!

Beatrice Schenk de Regniers

My dragon

My bath towel has a dragon
That's red and green and blue.
He has wings and breathes out fire
From his mouth and his nostrils too.

So every day at bath time
When I'm wet from top to toe,
I pretend my dragon dries me
With the fire from his nose.

Mary Dawson

Big and little

I'm littler than little,
I'm smaller than small,
I'm so very tiny, you can't see me at all.
Oh no you can't see me, but be sure I am here,
I'm the glint in your eye,
I'm the voice in your ear.

I'm bigger than big,
I'm huger than huge
I'm so very enormous, I can't even move.
But you know, you can't see me,
Though I'm everywhere,
I'm the heat of the sun,
I'm the light in the air.

Clive Riche

This is the key of the kingdom

This is the key of the kingdom:
In that kingdom is a city,
In that city is a town,
In that town there is a street,
In that street there winds a lane,
In that lane there is a yard,
In that yard there is a house,
In that house there waits a room,
In that room there is a bed,
On that bed there is a basket,
    A basket of flowers.

Flowers in the basket,
Basket on the bed,
Bed in the chamber,
Chamber in the house,
House in the weedy yard,
Yard in the winding lane,
Lane in the broad street,
Street in the high town,
Town in the city,
City in the kingdom:
    This is the key of the kingdom.

Anon

Pink azalea

I feel as though
this bush were grown
especially for me.
I feel as though
I almost am
this little flowering tree.

Charlotte Zolotow

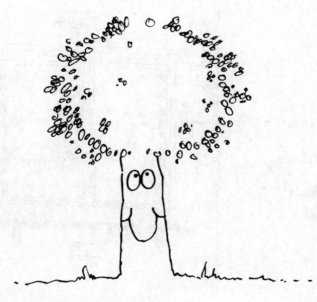

My shadow

As I walk home to have my tea,
My shadow walks along with me,
When I skip, then he skips too,
He copies everything I do.

I clap my hands, and his hands meet,
And just like me, he's got two feet,
I nod, he nods, it's such fun,
Playing with him in the sun.

As I walk home to have my tea,
The sun grows pale, and so does he,
And when the sun has gone from view,
I know that he will vanish, too.

Helen Russell

Yellow

Yellow for melons.
Yellow for sun.
Yellow for buttercups,
Picked one by one.

The yolk of an egg
Is yellow, too.
And sometimes clouds
Have a daffodil hue.

Bananas are yellow
And candleshine.
What's your favourite colour?
Yellow is mine.

Olive Dove

Peculiar

There's a strange looking creature at the
    corner of our street,
Dressed in red, he never moves, for he hasn't
    any feet;
His mouth is always open but he never says a
    word,
And appears to live on letters, which seems to
    me absurd.

Roland Egan

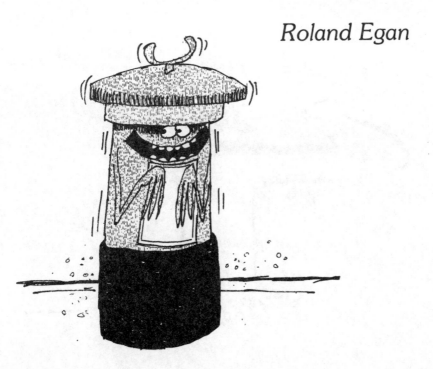

River winding

Rain falling, what things do you grow?
Snow melting, where do you go?
Wind blowing, what trees do you know?
River winding, where do you flow?

Charlotte Zolotow

If birds flew backwards

The goblin

A goblin lives in our house, in our house, in our
    house,
A goblin lives in our house all the year round.
    He bumps
    And he jumps
    And he thumps
    And he stumps.
    He knocks
    And he rocks
    And he rattles at the locks.
A goblin lives in our house, in our house, in our
    house,
A goblin lives in our house all the year round.

Rose Fyleman

138

The Goops

The Goops they lick their fingers,
And the Goops they lick their knives;
They spill their broth on the tablecloth –
Oh they lead disgusting lives!
The Goops they talk while eating,
And loud and fast they chew;
And that is why I'm glad that I
Am not a Goop – are you?

Gelett Burgess

Witch! Witch!

Witch, Witch,
where do you hide?

DOWN IN A DITCH
WHERE THE FROG-THINGS BIDE.

Witch, Witch,
what do you do?

I'M WEAVING A MAGICAL
SPELL OR TWO.

POP!

Witch, Witch,
what do you see?

A MILLION-AND-ONE-THINGS
THAT CAN'T SEE ME.

Witch, Witch,
when do you ride?

AT ONE-HOUR-TO-MIDNIGHT
ON HALLOWEEN-TIDE.

Ivy O. Eastwick

What a laugh!

I have a hen
    Who lays apples, not eggs!
I have a cat
    Who barks and begs!
I have a horse
    Who can balance on his nose
A big pink pig
    And two hippopotamose!
I have a short-necked,
    Tall giraffe.
And I have another thing –
    A JOLLY GOOD LAUGH!

Jenny Cornelius

Imagine

If the sea was in the sky,
And trees grew underground,
And if all fish had giant teeth,
And all the cows were round;
If birds flew backwards all the time,
And vultures ruled the land;
If bricks poured down instead of rain,
If all there was was sand;
If every man had seven heads
And we spoke Double Dutch,
And if the sun came out at night,
I wouldn't like it much.

Anon

Alligator

From Sydney Zoo
An Alligator
Was put on board
A flying freighter.
He ate the pilot
And the navigator
Then asked for more,
With mashed potater.

Spike Milligan

As I was going up the stair

As I was going up the stair
I met a man who wasn't there.
He wasn't there again today.
Oh, how I wish he'd go away!

Anon

Giant

A Giant
  is someone
    ten miles high
      whose feet
        touch the ground
          and whose head
            hits the sky.

And if I
  saw a Giant
    walking down
      our way
        I wouldn't stop
          but I'd run away
            and hide in a doorway
              quiet as a fly . . .

And I wouldn't come out till he'd gone by!

Ivy O. Eastwick

Did I ever tell you?

Did I ever tell you
of thin Mrs. Trimble?
She poured all her porridge oats
into a thimble.
She used for a ladle
the leg of a pin . . .
Now, is it surprising
so little went in?

Her bones were as small
as the bones of a linnet —
a pigeon could carry her
off in a minute . . .
A cockerel could carry her
off in a trice.
But nobody took her.
She wouldn't taste nice.

Jean Kenward

The scarecrow

There's a scarecrow in our garden
dressed in tatty clothes and rags
with a grinning knotty turnip
for a head.

There's something strange about it:
when I look out through the window
it's moved a little closer and it's
scaring me instead!

Adrian Rumble

The witch's brew

Into my pot there now must go
Leg of lamb and green frog's toe,

Old men's socks and dirty jeans,
A rotten egg and cold baked beans.

Hubble bubble at the double
Cooking pot stir up some trouble.

One dead fly and a wild wasp's sting,
The eye of a sheep and the heart of a king.

A stolen jewel and mouldy salt,
And for good flavour a jar of malt.

Hubble bubble at the double
Cooking pot stir up some trouble.

Wing of bird and head of mouse,
Screams and howls from a haunted house.

And don't forget the pint of blood,
Or the sardine tin and the clod of mud.

Hubble bubble at the double
Cooking pot stir up some TROUBLE!

Wes Magee

The clapping song

3 . . . 6 . . . 9
the goose drank wine
the monkey chewed tobacco
on a streetcar line.
The line broke
the monkey got choked
and they all went to heaven
in a little row boat.

Clap clap
clap hands.

My mother told me
if I was goody
she would buy me a rubber dolly.
My sister told her
I kissed a soldier
now she won't buy me a rubber dolly.

Clap clap
clap hands.

L. Chase

'Biby's' epitaph

A muvver was barfin' 'er biby one night,
The youngest of ten and a tiny young mite,
The muvver was poor and the biby was thin,
Only a skelington covered in skin;
The muvver turned rahnd for the soap off the rack,
She was but a moment, but when she turned back,
The biby was gorn; and in anguish she cried,
'Oh, where is my biby?' – The angels replied:

'Your biby 'as fell dahn the plug-'ole,
Your biby 'as gorn dahn the plug;
The poor little thing was so skinny and thin
'E oughter been barfed in a jug;
Your biby is perfeckly 'appy,
'E won't need a barf any more,
Your biby 'as fell dahn the plug-'ole,
Not lorst, but gorn before.'

Anon

We passed it on

Dad told Mum,
Mum told me,
I told the dog,
Who laughed 'Tee Hee,'
Dog told the pussycat,
Cat told the mouse,
Who called out as he scampered off,
'I'm glad you like your house.'

Helen Russell

Fifty cents

I asked my mother for fifty cents
To see the elephant jump the fence.

He jumped so high,
He reached the sky.

He never came back
'Til the Fourth of July.

Anon

We love him

We've got an elephant in our house,
He's far too big, you know,
We let him stay with us because,
He's got nowhere else to go.

I asked him how we got him,
He pretended not to hear,
So I expect we'll have to keep him,
For at least another year.

Of course we'd never throw him out,
For that would not be fair,
And all of us would miss him so,
If he wasn't there.

Helen Russell

Index of authors

Index of first lines

159

Acknowledgements

For permission to reproduce copyright material the editor is indebted to:
Abelard Schuman Ltd for *Pink Azalea, River Winding* and *Scene* by Charlotte Zolotow
from 'River Winding' and with Barbara Baker for *A spike of green* by Barbara Baker
from 'Poems and Pictures.' Dorothy Aldis and G. P. Putnam's Sons for *The clown* by
Dorothy Aldis from 'All Together'. William Cole Books for *Oh, who will wash the
tiger's ears* by Shel Silverstein. Dobson Books for *Alligator* and *Sardines* by Spike
Milligan from 'A Book of Milligan Animals'. E.M.I. Music Publishing Co. for *The
clapping song* by L. Chase. Alexander Franklin for *Open windows*. Hamish Hamilton
for *Bees* by Jack Prelutsky from 'Zoo Doings'. Hamlyn Publishing Group Ltd. for
Imagine and *The biggest firework* from 'Long, Short and Tall Tales' and for *Teddy
Bear* by L. H. Allen and *The Goops* by Gelett Burgess from 'Junket and Jumblies'.
Harcourt Brace Jovanovitch Inc. for *Sing a song of pockets* by Beatrice Schenk de
Regniers from 'Something Special' and with World Inc. for *Why did the children* by
Carl Sandburg from 'The People, Yes'. Harper and Bros. for *Engineers* by Jimmy
Garthwaite from 'Puddin' an' Pie'. Hodder and Stoughton Childrens Books for *Fly* by
Peggy Dunstan from 'In and Out of the Windows'. Macdonald Educational for *The
mammoth* and *Sabretooth* by Tom Stanier from 'Hocus Pocus Diplodocus'. Puffin
Books for *A thousand hairy savages* by Spike Milligan from 'Silly Verse for Kids'.
Sheldon Vidibor Inc. and Harper and Row for *Merry . . .* by Shel Silverstein from
'Where the Sidewalk Ends'. The Society of Authors for *The goblin* and *Hen's Song* by
Rose Fyleman and for *I meant to do my work today* by Richard le Gallienne. Stainer
and Bell Ltd for *Little Arabella Miller* by Ann Elliott from 'Fingers and Thumbs'. The
late Mrs. E. F. Starkey's estate for *A piper* by Seumas O'Sullivan. World's Work for *Up
in the air* by James S. Tippett from 'Crickety Cricket'. Every effort has been made to
trace the owners of copyrights, but we take this opportunity of tendering apologies to
any owners whose rights have been unwittingly infringed.